Toads

By Kari Schuetz

BELLWETHER MEDIA • MINNEAPOLIS, MN

Note to Librarians, Teachers, and Parents:

Blastoff! Readers are carefully developed by literacy experts and combine standards-based content with developmentally appropriate text.

Level 1 provides the most support through repetition of high-frequency words, light text, predictable sentence patterns, and strong visual support.

Level 2 offers early readers a bit more challenge through varied simple sentences, increased text load, and less repetition of high-frequency words.

Level 3 advances early-fluent readers toward fluency through increased text and concept load, less reliance on visuals, longer sentences, and more literary language.

Level 4 builds reading stamina by providing more text per page, increased use of punctuation, greater variation in sentence patterns, and increasingly challenging vocabulary.

Level 5 encourages children to move from "learning to read" to "reading to learn" by providing even more text, varied writing styles, and less familiar topics.

Whichever book is right for your reader, Blastoff! Readers are the perfect books to build confidence and encourage a love of reading that will last a lifetime!

This edition first published in 2012 by Bellwether Media, Inc.

No part of this publication may be reproduced in whole or in part without written permission of the publisher. For information regarding permission, write to Bellwether Media, Inc., Attention: Permissions Department, 5357 Penn Avenue South, Minneapolis, MN 55419.

Library of Congress Cataloging-in-Publication Data
Schuetz, Kari.
Toads / by Kari Schuetz.
   p. cm. – (Blastoff! readers. Backyard wildlife)
Includes bibliographical references and index.
Summary: "Developed by literacy experts for students in kindergarten through grade three, this book introduces toads to young readers through leveled text and related photos"–Provided by publisher.
ISBN 978-1-60014-724-1 (hardcover : alk. paper)
1. Toads–Juvenile literature. I. Title.
QL668.E2S38 2012
597.8'7–dc23   2011029688

Printed in the United States of America, North Mankato, MN.

010112   1207

Contents

Toads are **amphibians** with short legs and plump bodies. They have dry skin with warts.

Toads eat **insects**, spiders, and worms. They use their long tongues to catch quick **prey**.

Toads begin their lives as eggs in water. A group of eggs looks like a long chain.

Tadpoles hatch from the eggs. They have tails to swim. **Gills** help them breathe underwater.

gills

Tadpoles change into adult toads. They grow legs and **lungs**.

Legs let toads hop on land. Lungs let them breathe air.

Toads ooze **poison** from their skin when they face **predators**. It makes them taste bad.

They also puff
up their bodies
to look bigger.

Toads even
play dead to
fool predators.
Tricky toad!

Glossary

amphibians—animals that live both on land and in water

gills—body parts that let animals breathe underwater

insects—animals with six legs and hard outer bodies; insect bodies are divided into three parts.

lungs—body parts that let animals breathe on land

poison—something that can harm or kill

predators—animals that hunt other animals for food

prey—animals that are hunted by other animals for food

tadpoles—young toads; tadpoles live in water.

To Learn More

AT THE LIBRARY

Brown, Ruth. *Toad*. New York, N.Y.: Puffin Books, 1999.

Burns, Diane L. *Frogs, Toads, and Turtles*. Milwaukee, Wisc.: Gareth Stevens Pub., 2000.

Ryder, Joanne. *Toad by the Road: A Year in the Life of These Amazing Amphibians*. New York, N.Y.: H. Holt, 2007.

ON THE WEB

Learning more about toads is as easy as 1, 2, 3.

1. Go to www.factsurfer.com.

2. Enter "toads" into the search box.

3. Click the "Surf" button and you will see a list of related Web sites.

With factsurfer.com, finding more information is just a click away.

Index

The images in this book are reproduced through the courtesy of: Gail Shumway / Getty Images, front cover; Ellwood Eppard, pp. 5, 7 (right), 11; Shinji Kusano / Minden Pictures, p. 7 (top); Doug Lemke, p. 7 (left); Albie Venter, p. 7 (middle); Layer W / Photolibrary, p. 9; Brian Bevan / Ardea, p. 13; Rolf Nussbaumer / Alamy, p. 15; Paulo De Oliveira / Getty Images, p. 17; George McCarthy / naturepl.com, p. 19; Emanuele Biggi / Photolibrary, p. 21.